MISCONCEPTIONS ON THE USAGE OF JEWELRIES

AKINMEYE AKINBODE

ACKNOWLEDGEMENT

My profound appreciations to the Almighty God for his love and care. I also want to appreciate Bro Gbenga Odejide for his support to actualize this work. Bro Adejoro Emmanuel is not equally forgotten who assisted in the typesetting. The following people Bro Michael Godwin, Bro Samuel Oludare are appreciated for the contributions. God bless you all.

DEDICATION

The book is dedicated to my Joy Sis Akinmeye Oluwakemisola precious and my lovely children; Akintunde, Akinola and Akintomiwa. God bless you all.

INTRODUCTION

A man once came to Jesus and asked "Good teacher what must I do to inherit the kingdom of GOD?" In the book of Luke: 18vs18, Jesus answering him and said "you know GOD's commands; you must not do the sin of adultery, you must not murder anyone, you must not steal anything, you must not tell lies about other people, you must honor your parents. Jesus did not say you must not wear earrings or use gold.

The church of GOD today talks mostly on the use of gold and jewelries as if that takes you to hell but put aside that which populates hell per second. I have heard of many who claimed to have visited hell telling us that they saw people crying in hell just because of gold and jewelries. The book of Revelation 21vs8, talks about things that take a man to hell but it also did not include jewelry or gold. Does that mean the writer forgot to include it? GOD created all things and there was nothing created by GOD that He detests. It is only the wrong use or wrong application of things around us that provoke Him. John 1vs1-2 said all things were created by him and there was nothing created outside GOD. Why would GOD make something he hates?

Revelation 21vs 9-21 tells us of a beautiful apparatus used to design the New Jerusalem that we are expecting.

Verses 20-21 of the same Rev 21, talks about gold and other good looking materials created by GOD and that would be used also by GOD to design the New Jerusalem. If gold and jewelries were wrong in the present world, why would GOD talk of making the coming perfect world with what man (not GOD) terms evil.

Are you saying that GOD is repeating the mistakes He made for creating jewels of gold for man's use? If it were wrong then it is wrong now and it will be wrong to be in the coming Jerusalem.

Gold and silvers, wealth of the world and the world itself belong to GOD... Hagai 2:8; The earth is the Lord's and everything in it.

GOD cannot and does not hate anything he created not even Satan nor man, trees, stones, moons, sun and sea creatures. However, what we do with GOD's given gift, grace and ability in us determines His love and hatred.

Genesis 19vs1-29, describes the destruction of Sodom and its inhabitants. GOD destroyed the Sodomites and the city yet Lot and his daughters were saved to show that GOD did not hate the city and the Sodomites but they created enmity between themselves and GOD because of their foolish handling of GOD's given gift like their body.

Please read through the pages of this book to see and know what the scripture really says about gold and jewelry and not what man says.

CHAPTER ONE

FOREIGN GODS

Genesis 35vs1-4, GOD said to Jacob go to the town of Bethel, live there and make an altar for worship. Remember EL, the GOD who appeared to you when you were running away from your brother Esau, make your altar to worship that GOD there.

Vs 2, Jacob said to his family and to all his servants, remove all those foreign gods that you have, make yourself pure, put on clean cloth. Vs 3; We will leave here and go to bethel in that place I will build an altar to the GOD who helped me in time of trouble and that GOD has been with me everywhere I went.

Vs 4; so the people gave Jacob all the foreign gods that they had. And they gave Jacob all the rings that they were wearing in their ears. Jacob buried all these things under an oak tree near the town called Shechem.

GOD said to Jacob, go to bethel, make an altar there and worship GOD who appeared to you. And Jacob not GOD said give me the foreign gods in your possession. Where did they get the foreign gods? Of course in Laban's house where they were born and raised, Idolatry was permitted and they were trained in the ways of idols.

These people were coming from the house of an idol worshipper, a descendant of Terah the father of

Abraham

Gen 11:27.

Joshua 24:2;

Joshua spoke to all the people, he said I am telling you what the Lord, the GOD of Israel says to you: a long time ago your ancestors lived on the other side of the Euphrates River. I am talking about men like Terah; the father of Abraham and Nahor. At that time, those men worshipped other gods.

Vs:3a; But I the LORD took your father Abraham out of the land on the other side of the river.

Terah was a full idol worshipper who trained his children in the way of his idol but Abraham was different and GOD separated him in order to raise His own children in the way of the LORD. Abraham raised Isaac and Isaac raised Jacob, Rachel and Leah on the other hand were raised by Laban, an idolater.

Jacob knew that idolatry was a terrible sin in the sight of the GOD of Israel.

Exodus 20 V 3&4 says you must not worship other god except me.

WHY DID JACOB COLLECT THEIR IDOLS AND THE JEWELS OF GOLD?

These idols were made of gold and jewelries. If Jacob permitted them to go with their jewelries, they will make for themselves gods after their hearts likeness for they only left Laban's house but still carried about the doctrines and systems and beliefs they had. Laban raised them, taught them and they carry that around.

> **Genesis31:14-15;**
>
> **Rachel and Leah answered Jacob, our father has nothing to give us when he dies, he treated us like strangers, sold us to you, spent what is ours and GOD took all this wealth from our father and now it belongs to us and our children, do whatever GOD told you to do.**

Rachel mentioned in her speech that it was GOD that blessed Jacob by collecting parts of Laban's wealth and gave it to Jacob. It means that what Laban worshiped is not GOD but Jacob had found the way of the true GOD and Jacob did not talk to GOD through any medium but in faith without images but she cannot easily do away with what she leant from her father's house. They agreed to follow Jacob in body but their hearts could not be with Jacob.

> **Genesis31:19;**
>
> **At this time, Laban was gone to cut wool from his sheep. While he was gone, Rachel went into**

his house and stole the false gods that belonged to her father.

Rachel stole her father's idols because her heart was still in the way Laban raised her. She believed in Laban's gods which is a detestable thing to GOD. She believed in vain things rather than in GOD whose works proves his existence.

Leah and Rachel had been wearing jewels of gold for years in their father's house but at the time when they needed to go to bethel for worship, Jacob requested for their idol and jewel of gold. We have people today that stand on this verse of the Bible; they wear jewelries at home and put it away when going to the church. Anything that is wrong in the church is wrong at home. What defies you in the church defies you at home. Why will GOD be angered by jewelries and gold when He is the creator of all things. If Jacob had not collected the jewels of gold from his family, they would have placed it down at bethel to worship. They were trained to worship GOD with visible images unlike Jacob who believed that worship requires faith not sight. Learn from Gideon in the book of

Judges 8:24

Gideon said unto them, I would desire a request of you that you would give me every man the earrings of his prey {for they had golden earrings because they were

Ishmaelites.

Verse 25-26 says; they dropped with Gideon gold and earring and verse 27 says; Gideon used the gold to make an ephod. He put the ephod in his home town called Ophrah, all the people of Israel worshiped the ephod. In this way the people of Israel were not faithful to GOD and the ephod became a trap that caused Gideon and his family to sin.

GOD was not angry with them for holding the jewels of gold, HE was not angry with them for making Ephod but for worshiping the ephod, giving glory to vein things rather than to the ONLY GOD.

If Jacob did not collect the Jewels of gold and the gods, they would worship it for what they went there for is to worship. Jacob saw ahead the danger of allowing them to go with jewels to Bethel and he prevented it. If jewelries are wrong in Bethel then it is wrong in the market square and at home. God hates hypocrisy. Someone said gold and jewelries are for the gentiles for they mentioned Ishmaelites.

> **Exodus 3:21**
>
> **God said to Moses, that I will cause the Egyptian people to be kind to the people of Israel. The Egyptians will give many gifts to your people when they leave Egypt.**

GOD THE ONLYAND HOLY Person in heaven and on earth said 'I will not let you go empty-handed but will grant you favor in Egypt and the Egyptians will give you gifts.

It is only a religious mind that will not want to see this powerful statement. Do you think that God would give us a serpent or stone instead of food Luke 11:13 says:

Man is evil but God is good and he would not give you what will kill you. Far be it that God should do that.

Brethren, let's see what God promised to give to his people after four hundred years (400yrs) of service in Egypt. Verse 22 of Exodus 3;

God said that all of the Hebrew women should ask their Egyptian neighbors living in their houses for gift. And those Egyptian women will give you gifts of silver, gold and fine clothing.

God told the Hebrews to ask of gold from the Egyptians, the very same thing which Jacob collected from his people and some termed it to be evil. If gold use meant idolatry then that means that God is engracing them to do evil. Far be it that God should do that.

God's word stand for ever, Jacob was the father of Israel who collected the gold and jewelries. Then, a few hundred years later GOD said I will give you favor to receive gifts of the same gold. Why will GOD put a stumbling block on His children' path? If you my reader know that GOD cannot do evil and cannot give serpent to His children then asking the Egyptians for gold is a living proof that gold was never wrong.

GOD did not initially ask Jacob to withdraw the jewelries but Jacob was well trained to know that GOD is a jealous GOD therefore; one must not place before Him an image of any kind to worship. He thus foresaw the danger of them going to Bethel with their jewelries that was why he withdrew the gold along with the idols for they could make the same idol with their jewelry being what they knew best to do.

Rachael stole her father's idol and her husband Jacob did not know until the deed was done and declared death on whoever stole the gods. Jacob got to know about it later. Are you saying that Jacob did not know? How did you have the record, if Jacob did not get to know and on their way for settlement Rachael died. This woman did not consult Jacob before taking the idol hence if the gold jewelry was not withdrawn, she may not tell Jacob before making images.

Man cannot boast of a woman whose heart is not fully with him. She may be with you in body and not with you in heart but GOD was asking for Adam's heart. You can be present in church and not be in HIS Presence. God said {not man},I will give you favor to request for gifts from the gentiles. GOD loves the world, Nigeria, Ghana and Egypt as HE loved Israel. HE created the world and you only live in a small part of the world. GOD created whatever you touch around you AND HE CANNOT BE ANGRY FOR MERELY TOUCHING AND USING THEM BUT THE ABUSIVE USAGE OF THEM ALL MAKES GOD SAD..

WHAT WOULD THEY USE IT FOR
EXODUS 3:22

...and ye shall put them upon your children.
You will put those gifts on your children. The passage says
they shall carry part of the Egyptians' wealth because gold
is a costly treasure till date. Putting it on their children may
still make religious minds to argue that it is not to their
ears. However, Genesis 35:4 said they gave to Jacob all the
rings they were wearing in their **EARS. Also**

**Exodus 32:2; And Aaron said bring the gold
earrings that belong to your wives, your sons
and of your daughters and bring them unto
me.**

Women did not just start using earring in our age but
GOD said put it on your children and verse 2 of Exodus
chapter 32 shows us that they had earrings and God was
not angry with them.

The GOD of Jacob is the GOD of Moses and our GOD. If
jewels of gold were wrong in the time of Jacob then it is
wrong in the time of Moses. Brethren don't judge things
blindly all because it is a public saying; A wise man correct
mistakes. A man that corrects mistakes must be prudent.

Exodus 11:2-3

You must give this message to the people of Israel: men and women, you must ask your neighbors to give you things made of silver and gold (Vs:3): the LORD will cause the Egyptians to be kind to you (Israel).

The Egyptians even pharaoh's own officials already considered Moses to be a great man. This chapter proved that chapter 3 was not a typographical mistake but confirmed words of GOD. Moses said don't forget to ask your neighbours for gifts made of gold and silver. Perhaps they asked, how will it be possible? He said for the mighty HAND OF GOD will grant you kindness and compel these people to give you whatever you ask them.

GOD was not seeing gold and silver and jewelries made of them as evil and that was why HE instructed them to leave Egypt with treasures and put it on their children and not to keep it in their wardrobe or to hide it but to put it on their children.

Are you saying these chapters are dogma? If no, then, believe what you read in the bible. Things that Jesus said are wrong are the things we do and we don't teach our members to abstain from them.

We don't accurately and consciously live by it but we teach members tribal traditions and create unnecessary consciousness of the irrelevant.

Are you the type that wears no earring but fornicates? It is easier for mere men to be deceived by your looks but GOD sees your heart, your hidden activities and He cannot be deceived.

Favoured Indeed

Exodus: 12: 35–36

(35) Then the people of Israel did what Moses assured them to do. They went to their Egyptian neighbours and asked for clothing and things made from silver and gold (vs 36) And THE LORD caused the Egyptian to be kind to the people of Israel. So the Egyptian gave their riches to the people of Israel.

Days after, GOD did what he said. A man can realize within hours of his mistake, how much more GOD; who can never and will never make mistakes. GOD proved the word to be divine to the Israelites by making their neighbor to submit to them treasures' of silver and gold.

The Egyptians had food and useful animal that the Israelites needed but GOD said ask for gold and silver and things made of them and clothing, then, put it on your children. The phrase "put it on your children" occurs several times to show that they are to be wearing it not to keep it.

CHAPTER TWO

ISRAEL REMOVED THEIR GOLD RING

Exodus, 38; 4

The people heard this bad news and became very sad and the people stopped wearing jewelries because the LORD said to Moses, Tell the people of Israel you are a stubborn people. I might destroy you even if I travel with you only a short time. So take off all your jewelry while I decide what to do with you (vs 6) so the people of Israel stopped wearing jewelry at mount Horeb

(Sinai).

NOTE: GOD said Remove it

   GOD said they are stubborn

   GOD said He might destroy them.

Removing the jewelry sounds like it was a mistake. However, there won't be need for a change if there are no reasons.

Exodus, 32:1 the people saw that a long time had passed and Moses had not come down from the mountain. So the people gathered around Aaron. They said to him. "Look, Moses led us out of the land of Egypt. But we don't know what has happened to him. So make us some gods to go before us and lead us."

(vs 2) Aaron said to the people bring me the gold earrings that belong to your wives, sons and daughters.

(vs 3) All the people gathered their gold earrings and brought them to Aaron.

(vs.4) Aaron took the gold from the people. And he used it to make a statue of a calf. Then, the people said, Israel here are your gods that brought you out of the land of Egypt.

The Israelites wore earrings and GOD was not angry but at a time they went against his commands like I said earlier, wrong handling of GOD given gifts provoke GOD.

 GOD said wear the things made of gold and silver on your children. The people said make for us a god to go before us. How can what you make go before you? How can what you carry lead you? This is enough to provoke GOD. They blindly imagined that the gold images can lead. Despite the great manifestation of wonders they saw God did in Egypt and at the red sea, they didn't believe in Moses and Aaron but in gold images. The Israelites had lived with the Egyptians for years. They were there; saw the social and religious activities and they inculcated the habit. They only followed Moses just like Rachel followed Jacob but still held on to the Egyptian beliefs.

(verse 6) The people woke up very early the next morning. They killed animals and offered them as burnt offerings and fellowship offerings.

Every ceremonial activity recorded here were things they saw in Egypt and it provoked GOD. They danced before a mere image made by man;

(verse 9) The LORD said to Moses. I have seen these people. I know that they are very stubborn people. They will always turn against Me (10) so now let me destroy them in anger then, I will make a great nation from you.

Saying "They are stubborn" means that they left God laid down rules and went after their fleshy wishes; being stubborn or stiff necked means disobedience

GOD said collect things made of gold and put it on your children but they removed it and made a golden calf of it and worshipped it. When you are asked to touch but you push, you have disobeyed and that is stubbornness. GOD was angry not because they wore gold but because they removed it and made Images they called gods.

(Verse 22)Aaron In his own mortal defense, said don't be angry sir. You know that these people are always ready to do wrong.

These people are always ready to go their way, to do their desire, to follow their old doctrines, to use GODS given gifts in a wrong way that provoked GOD. They are not laws abiding followers.

A child that does his father's will is said to be faithful and obedient but when he goes his own way, then, he is stubborn and disobedient.

I told the people, give me your gold rings and the people gave me their gold. I threw the gold into the fire and out of the fire came this calf. Judge for yourselves. Was it the gold rings or the calf that provoked GOD. It was the people's decision of provoking GOD by going against him {exodus,32:24}.

Exodus 20: 3- 4 said, thou shall not worship any other gods except me.

(4) Thou shall not make any idols, status of anything up in the sky or in the earth or water.

Worship is meant only for GOD and no other one not even angels are worthy of worship. If angels that GOD created and endowed with grace and power would not be worshipped then what is man and the dead works of man is to be worshipped. This is an insult and a total description of the Hebrew mental bondage. The Egyptians did not just enslave them but also enslaved their mental strengths.

THEY CHOSE DARKNESS

Though, GOD allowed the Hebrews to see light in Egypt, He performed wonders that no man could perform. He made known the uselessness of the Egyptian gods and magicians. He killed and in the same place spared them. He announced their freedom and that night they were freed. Despite all these, they chose darkness. They still remembered the religious activities of the Egyptians and could not remember what GOD used Aaron to do with the staff in Egypt and learn that, what they needed was GOD and Aaron His prophet was there with them.

REMOVE FROM YOU (Exodus,33:4-5)

God said take off all your jewelry while I decide what to do with you and the people stopped wearing their jewelry at mount Horeb. God said something different here, God said remove from you your gold ring. Same God who said request for things made of gold, put it on your children, now said remove it.

Note one thing here" If God was angry with the wearing of gold, He would have said collect it from them all and dispose them but God only said remove it. For instance; a child offended his father and ran to call an elder to appeal, his father said go out first, that does not mean the child will not enter into the house again. God was angry and he said "I might destroy you if I go with you", seeing them with gold ring on them easily shows what they have done with it. God sees without light yet he wanted them to remove it and they did. It was a test and they passed. Note this in verse 6 of Exodus chapter 33, and they stopped wearing gold ring at mount Horeb.

This verse did not say that they stopped wearing gold ring forever or from that day but at mount Horeb (Sinai) throughout the time they lived on mount Hereb, they did not wear gold rings. But does it mean they did not wear it anymore?

I remember my secondary school days when a student brought a toy that disturbed the class during a teaching class session. The teacher was angry and asked the boy to keep it. The boy kept it until the teacher left but he still played with the toy after. It was not the toy the teacher detested but the wrong time he played with it, for he disrespected the teacher.

God said remove it, He never said throw it away or burn it or sell it but remove it until I decide what to do with you. When you are asked to remove the cup that is on the table and you remove it, won't you make use of the cup again? God did say remove it and the scripture says they stopped wearing gold ring at mount Horeb.

GIFTS FOR THE BUILDING OF THE TEMPLE

Exodus 35:4

Moses said to all the people of Israel, this is what they commanded; gather special gifts for the Lord. Each of you should decide in your heart what you will give. And then you should bring that gold to the Lord. Bring gold, silver and bronze (6) blue, purple and red yarn and fine linen, goat hair. Ram skins, dyed red and fine leather. Note: This is what the Lord commanded, it was after they left mount Horeb, that God Said bring gifts like, gold, silver and others, it means God had no problems with gold. It was the worshipping of the calf image that provoked HIM. Gold was part of things used to build the holy tents and also the apocalypse tell us that the New Jerusalem was made of pure gold, as pure as glass.

Things made of a very expensive tents and the tent was holy with the gold and silver and expensive sweet smelling incense. Please, holiness is not rough dressing. Putting on something good does not mean you are for hell. Hell is a cursed place prepared for the cursed. Gold is not cursed and cannot be found in hell, gold and the uses of things made of gold cannot take you to hell but the breaking of God given commandments. Jesus says in the book of john 15:17, This is my command, love each other, your relationship to others is what determined your destination, not gold, you may not put on jewelry but you lies, you steal, you fornicate and hell will celebrate your arrival, 1 Cor. 6:9.

Surely you know that the people that do wrong will not get into Gods kingdom. Don't be fooled, these people will not enter into Gods kingdom. People that sin sexually, people that worship idols, people that commit the sin of adultery, greedy people, drunkards, people that say bad things of others.

You are conscious of what you wear but unconscious of what you do. You are what you do and what you do is what you are judged with. You may be judged for eating food. It is not the food that provoked GOD but how you get it (e.g. if you stole the food) God judges your decisions and thoughts. David slept with Bathsheba and God was seriously angry with David. God was not angry for sleeping with Bathsheba but God was angry for sleeping with another man's wife. If David had married Bathsheba before Uriah, no problem, after all God was not angry that David slept with Michal. God created man with manhood and woman with womanhood should we cut manhood of a man because it makes him vulnerable to temptations. If we will not cut what makes you a man then stopping the wearing of earring is not the solution to idolatry.

God said bring gifts for the building of the Holy lands, Exodus35:4-5.No man gives what he does not have. If removing of your jewels means throwing away your jewels, how would they have given such as at when needed for the building of the temple? The wearing of earrings was stopped on mount Sinai but later used to build a tent for worship, because they are moving away from the mountain and Moses needed a holy place where they could still be meeting with God. Therefore God said, tell them to bring gifts such as required and they brought it Exo,35:29.

The children of Israel brought a willing offering unto the Lord, every man and woman whose heart made them willing to bring for all manner of work, which the Lord had commanded to be made by the hand of Moses.
If uses of jewelries of gold and silver were evil, God wouldn't have requested the Israelites to bring gifts like gold and silver.

Moses who wrote the law never said: "don't wear jewelries." Moses did not say, thou shall not wear jewelries but he said thou shall not fornicate. We don't talk about sexual immorality that is rampant today but we talk about gold. In your house and churches you have elements made of gold, your wedding ring slipping to your finger should be removed if gold ornamentation is wrong.

Exodus 35:31&32

THE LORD filled Bezalel with the SPIRIT OF GOD, who gave him special skill and knowledge to do all kinds of things (32) He design and make things with gold.

*Judge this: THE SPIRIT OF GOD gave the knowledge to work all kinds with gold

THE EPHOD

Exodus 28:1

The lord said to Moses, tell your brother, Aaron and his sons, Nadab, Abihu, Eleazer and Ithamarto come to you from the people of Israel.

These men will serve me as priests.

(vs2) Make special clothes for your brother Aaron these clothes will give him honor and respect.

(3)   There are skilled men among the people who can make these clothes. I have given these men special wisdom. These clothes will show that he served me in a special way.

(4)   These are the clothes the men should make the judgment pouch (The Ephod) a blue robe, a white woven robe, a turban and sash {belt}

(5)   Tell the men to use gold threads and fine linen and blue, purple and red yarn

(6)   Use gold threads, from linen and blue purple and red yarn to make the ephod

(8) The men will carefully weave a sash (belt) for the ephod. It must be made the same way as the ephod. Use gold threads

(14) Twist chains of pure gold together like a rope. Make two of these gold chains and fasten them to the gold setting.

Back to (vs 12), Aaron wore this special coat when he stood before the Lord. The Ephod was a special coat worn by the PRIESTS.

The priests were expensively dressed in a special way to serve before the special Holy and Only God.

They may make a golden setting and joined with a golden sash (belt) and pure gold chains.

A golden calf that was made by Aaron contributed by the Israelites provoked God because of wrong motives and purpose. Now, a coat attached with pure gold sash and chains, made the priests serve special before the Holy God

A GOLDEN BELL

(VS 37)

And beneath upon the hem of it, thou shall make pomegranates of blue, and of purple and of scarlet round about the hem thereof: and bell of gold between them round about. A bell that is purely gold was made for the priest.

PRIESTS WITH GOLD RING

Chains of pure gold were given to the priests attached to the ephod. Priests are specially selected people to enter the HOLY Of HOLIES of the temple, standing before God for worship. If gold and things of gold was wrong, how could God say make for my priests sash of gold, bell of gold and even the ephod.

People of Israel brought these gifts for the building of the temple and for the priestly garments.

THE ALTAR FOR BURNING INCENSE

Exodus 37: 25

He made the altar for burning incense, from acacia wood. The altar was square; it was 1 cubit long, 1 cubit wide and 2 cubits high. There were four horns on the altar, there was one horn on each corner, and these horns were joined together with the altar to make one piece

(26) He covered the top and on the sides and the horns with pure gold. Then he put gold from around the altar

(27) He made two gold rings for the altar. He put the gold ring below the each side of the altar.

These gold rings held the poles for carrying the altar.

David said if I regard iniquity in my heart, THOU LORD will not hear me. If gold means idolatry, then the incenses offered will be rejected but God accepted their offering with the burning altar of two long gold rings, holding the poles carrying the altar. The children of Israel donated those rings and Moses said unto them that they have provided more than was needed.

Verse 3 of chapter 36; All the skilled workers left the work they were doing on the Holy place and they went to speak to Moses

(5)   The people have brought too much, we have more than we need to finish the work on the tent

(6)   Then Moses sent this message throughout the camp, No man or woman should make anything else as a gift for the holy place. So the people were forced to stop giving more. Everything used for the building of the Holy Tents and things in it were the provisions supplied by

33

the Hebrew. If they had thrown away the things of gold collected in Egypt, there would have been need for God to create and miraculously provide for the making of His temple. The Israelites only removed the jewels of gold at Horeb. This then became useful for the building. They used jewels of gold to make Ephod and the priest wore it to the Holy of Holies in the presence of God and God was not provoked for seeing chains of gold and bell of pure gold and sash of gold nor the Ephod. Previously, we have seen how God was angry with Gideon's family and the Israelites not for making of ephod but for worshipping of ephod. Gideon made the ephod with the things of gold donated by the Hebrews though it is spoils from the Ishmaelites, the Ishmaelites were never the issue but the idolatry hearts and actions.

CHAPTER THREE

ISAIAH'S PROPHECY

Gen 35: 2

Then, Jacob said unto his household, and to all that were with him, put away the strange gods that are among you and be clean, and change your garments

(4) And they gave unto Jacob all the strange gods which were in their hand, and all their earrings which were in their ears and Jacob hid them under the oak which was by shechem.

From the verse, Jacob requested for strange gods and they gave up every form of gold in their possessions. Jacob collected everything that has to do with gold so that they will not make idols of it and provoke God so, should we also stop wearing earrings and gold rings so that we would not make idols?

35

Isaiah 44: 12;

The smith with the tongs both worketh in the coals and fashioneth it with hammers and worshippeth it with the strength of his arm: he is hungry, and his strength faileth; he drinketh no water and is faint.

He heweth him down cedars and taketh the cypress and the oak which he strengthened for himself among the trees of the forest.

Heplanteth an ash, and the rain doth nourish it.

They made gods with gold metal.

Verse 15;they made gods with wood. In our time, where it is rare to find gold and very rare to see smiths, people used wood to make gods for themselves, I have seen many images made of wood and placed in a corner to be worshipped, how can wood you cut& design, lead you.

(Verse 15); Then shall it be for a man to burn, for he will take hereof and warm himself, yea, he kindleth it and baketh bread; yes, he maketh a god and worshipeth it: he maketh it a graven image and falleth down thereto.

Based on some people's belief that any form of gold must not be worn because Jacob collected the strange gods and the people gave up all their jewelries. Then in our age, people should stop using wooden materials because people use it to make idols, Chairs and tables, wardrobes and other wooden materials must be removed because it is idolatry. Poverty makes idols worshipers to use wood as they cannot afford gold. If you say you don't use wood for idolatry but for cooking, making of chairs to sit on, et cetera. God in like manner created gold for our use and not for making idols. Those who idolized it would be punished as those who idolized wood must be surely punished.

I met a man years back and I saw him crafting a wooden image and saying he is making a female god for his male wooden idol. That is evil and highly detestable to God. Yet, we cannot stop people from using other wooden materials.

ISAIAH PROPHECY

Isa 3:17; My Lord will make sores on the heads of these women in Zion. The Lord will make the women lose all their hair

(18)   At that time, the Lord will take away all the things they are proud of; the beautiful ankle bracelets, the necklaces that look like the sun and the moon

(19)   The earrings, bracelets and veils (face covering) the scarves, the ankle chains.

The sashes worn around their waists, the bottle of perfume and the charms.

Many people conclude that this book shows that God hates earring).

Isaiah talks about veil and that they will lose their hair. Does it mean God is angry with women's hair or the veil that the Hebrews used which we do in our wedding engagements today? The scarves we use when praying was discussed here as one of the things that would be taken away.

Verses 22 and 23 of Isaiah talk about shawls for covering and purses that you take for outing and (23) talks about mirrors and turbans.

Why do people agree that this chapter is discussing about the earring and bracelets to be a wrong thing. If it is wrong, then, purses and mirrors are also wrong including scarves. Those who preach from this chapter on the altar will not speak against the scarves, the mirrors and the purses.

For how long do we tarry in Hypocrisy? Preach Jesus and what God desires of us and stop condemning what God created.

Ezekiel 16:5;

Jerusalem, you were all alone, no one felt sorry for you or take care of you. Jerusalem on the day you were born, your parents threw you out in the field. You were still covered with the blood and after birth.

(Verse 6) Then, I GOD passed by I saw you lying there, kicking in the blood. You covered with blood but I said please live!

39

(10)   I gave you a nice dress and soft leather shawls. I gave you a linen headband and a silk scarf

(11)   Then I gave you some jewelry. I put bracelets on your arm and a necklace around your neck

(12)   I gave you a nose ring, some earrings and a beautiful crown to wear

(13)   You were beautiful in your silver and gold jewelry and your linen, silk and embroidered material. You ate the best food, you were very beautiful and you became the queen.

God said I gave you all these to make you beautiful and he dressed the people so well but they did something that provoked God. It wasn't the earrings, nose rings or bracelets that provoked GOD but it was what they used it for

WHAT CAUSED THE PROPHESY

Isaiah 3:16;

The Lord says, the women in Zion have become very proud. They walk around with their heads in the air, acting like they are better than other people. Those women flirt with their eyes and they dance around making noise with their ankle bracelets.

Where you see the word PRIDE you know that the people have overestimated the value of the materials. They do not acknowledge God and they show to the people around the beauty of their ankle bracelets and making their hair beautiful and eyes well painted just to entice and seduce men because they dressed in the way of idol worshipers who engage in sexual immorality before their so called gods. They felt too important to obey the rules and regulations of the Holy temple. If God was having issues with earrings because it is stated here then, it is wrong to have veils, scarves and hair because we have them stated there but verse 16 says because they have become very proud.

Ezekiel 16:15; God said, but you began to trust in your beauty, you used the good name you had and became unfaithful to me, you acted like a prostitute with every man that passed by

41

(16)   you took your beautiful clothes and used them to decorate your places of worshiper

(17)   you took your beautiful jewelry that I gave you, and used that gold and silver to make status of men. And you had sex with them too.

(18)   you took the beautiful cloth and made clothes for these status, you took the perfume and incense I gave you and you put it in front of these idols

(19)   I gave you bread, honey and oil but you gave that food to your idols.

God said I gave you these things to make you look so beautiful. Did you notice the word? "I gave", "I gave", if you have a problem with this word then you have problem with the writer, prophet Ezekiel. A man of God that tells us more about what went wrong among the Hebrews. It is not the gold or its uses that provoked God but it is the wrong way of using it.

(1)   **FOR SEDUCTION:** Ladies dress today when they are going out but at home they may not take their bath

when they are still with their husband. You should dress to look good to your husband but if it is only used when going out then it is for seduction. Am I saying that you should not use it when going out, No, but use it most when around your husband and not to seduce men. Like the Hebrew women did that provoked God

Motive: why did you buy it? Is it to look sexy like Sister Mary.

Sexy means you are romantically attractive. Making strange men feeling sexually attracted to you, like some learn walking steps today, why do you think you need a special way of walking and what would it add to your life or remove from it? Whatever you do in the systems of the world without a genuine reason is questionable. There is nothing wrong with what God created but it is the wrong usage of it that is wrong. Should we cut off our manhood because of immorality, NO! Then, we should not condemn earrings but use it for what is good.

(2)   **IDOLATRY**: Like Isaiah said in Isa 44:12, 13 and 14. About what they used to make idols, gold, string line and wood. In our time, wood graving image is very common because they cannot afford gold. Should we stop people

from using gold because of fear of idolizing it, if yes, then, we should stop people from using wooden materials. If you can't stop wooding materials then you shouldn't stop gold usage but let us preach Gospel to people about what God wants and his gift which is JESUS, then, we will be reducing the numbers in hell and increasing the number in heaven. People don't see lies as a dangerous act, stealing, fornication and idolatry that is why they come to church with no earring but with evil in their hearts our members appear with no earrings and we believe they are saved, we don't bother to preach to them about the dangers of the manifestation of flesh Instead we preach against churches that wear earrings. Satan caused division among the church of God because he knows without unity we achieve less. Let the church of God realize this and fight against the devices of Satan to take the gospel away from our mouth. What saves is the gospel not preaching of earring but to tell the world that the KINGDOM OF GOD IS AT HAND.

Matt 28: 19.

Go ye therefore and teach all nations, baptizing them in the name of the FATHER and of the SON and of the HOLY

SPIRIT (20) Teaching them to observe all things, whatsoever I have commanded you: and I am with you always even unto the end of the world. Amen.

Teaching them to observe all things I had commanded you. Did HE mention earring? NO. That which HE asked us to keep, we break it, He taught us to love and be faithful to others. When you serve GOD faithfully then you will love and be good to men the works of His Hand.

CHAPTER FOUR

GOLD RING IN JOB TREACHERY

JOB 42:11

Then all of job's brothers and sisters and all of the people that knew job before came to his house. They all ate a big meal with job. They comforted job. They were sorry that the LORD had brought so much trouble to job. Each person gave job a piece of silver and a gold ring.

WHO IS JOB?

Job was one of the Arabian patriarchs that lived among the Hebrew with a vivid record that he served GOD with all his heart.

Job 1:1

There was a man named job that lived in the county of Uz. Job was a good and faithful man. Job worshiped God and refused to do evil to do evil things.

The Bible gave us the summary of job's attitude towards GOD. He was amongst other attributes, a good and faithful man. A good man as implied here means that job was a God fearing man that showed kindness to people around him

In reference to him being faithful man: Job was faithful to GOD such that he does everything as though GOD were right there before him. He kept to the rules and never went against the commandment of GOD. He would NOT Cheat his brethren and would not desire another man's wife. Notice also that job was a very wealthy man, and a man of influence yet there was no record of him having two wives. He lived the life of a priest of GOD, though a gentile by birth was a godly person by living.

Job worshipped GOD and refuses to do evil

Psalm 24: 3

Who can go up the LORDS Mountain?

Who can stand and worship, in the LORDS Holy

Temple

(Verse 4) People who have not done evil things

People who have pure hearts

People who have not used my name to make a lie sound like the truth

47

People who have not lied and made fake promises. Only these people can worship there. Job knew the disposition of God towards uprightness, little wonder in verse 5 of the book of job. Chapter 1 says, job got up early in the morning after his children had a party and offered a burnt offering for each of his children. He thought "maybe my children were careless and sinned against GOD at their party". Job always did this so his children would be forgiven of their sins.

Job knew that no impurity can be in his presence not in the centre called church. It takes a man of purity to worship in His TRUE presence. A man that is not deceiving himself must be pure in heart. Job offered sins offering to GOD for his children so that they would not live a second in sin.

The bible says that, job always did the burnt offering to GOD. Job's heart was full of GOD and he was careful with what he did so he would not provoke GOD to anger.

Why Did Job Collect Jewelry

Job 42:11 says that the family of job brought gifts to job, gifts of a piece of silver and gold ring.

A piece of silver was not one silver but a keshitah" this was a measure that was used in the time of the patriarchs {see Gen3: 19 and Joshua 24: 32}.

A man that was so careful in the things he daily did and even careful of the life that his children lived wouldn't have collected the gifts given to him by his brothers and sisters that traveled for comfort

They enriched job the more with money and gold which is a great investment with high value. Anybody that wear gold shows that he is rich and Job collected the gifts of silver and gold. We all preach today of job's faithfulness to GOD and his total surrender of all to GOD. If gold ring were wrong then job was wrong to have collected it. If however you believe that Job was a righteous man then his receiving of gift of gold rings was not wrong.

The same gold that Jacob collected and hid, Job collected for use. It is not the gold ring that is mainly the problem but what we do with it. Our eyes are mainly for good but we can decide to use it wrongly by looking lustfully at a woman. Job's children took turns having parties and job did not offer burnt offering because they partied, as though the party was wrong but because they may likely have done wrong things in the course of the party. The jewelry that is wonderfully made of GOD couldn't have been wrong in the sight of the maker but what we use it for will determine the heart of GOD towards us.

GOD'S CONFESSIONS ABOUT JOB

Job 1:8
Then the Lord said to Satan, "have you seen my servant? There is no person on earth like job. Job is a good and faithful man.

He worships GOD and refuses to do evil things. When God said that job was a faithful man and that he refuses to do evil. He implied that Job would not because of shame or respect for man do what is evil in the sight of God. Job was a man of high respect to the Lord and would not break that strong bond of relationship between him and God. Hence, Job knew that the gifts of earrings given to him by his relatives could not distant him from God because gold was never from the pit of Hell. HELL does not have any ability to create but Satan only leverage on our desire. If Satan can create earring then he can create his own world but he does not have

the ability to create. **John, 1:3 said that all things were created by the word of God and nothing else that was created after him.** Why then do you refer to gold ring as if it is from the pit of hell? Some even have hatred for it so much as if GAL; 5:19 INCLUDED IT... If we can have hatred for the many ills that we do every day in such manner that we have for gold, then, we will freely be in his presence. Some people don't know the gospel but they preach against wearing of earrings to people and the church. Yet, they use wedding rings and wrist watches as if Isaiah did not talk about it. If you are familiar with what you have previously read, then, you will understand what God was saying through, Isaiah and Ezekiel.

WHAT DID JOB DO WITH THE GOLD RING?

The books of Genesis, exodus, Isaiah and Ezekiel makes us to know that the Israelites wore earrings and job had daughters. In fact, the bible says they were very beautiful

51

than others. I am quite sure that job did not hide the gold ring but gave it to his daughters to make them look beautiful, not to seduce men.

Seduction is a thing of the heart; you can seduce men with mere looking or smiling without showing your nakedness. Therefore, God will judge us by what we think and do. If you go to hell because of a thing, it is not because the thing was wrong but because you wrongly used it. No fornicator will enter into the kingdom. What does he fornicate with? His manhood! Does it then mean that the man entered into hell because he had manhood? No, but for using it wrongly and for a wrong purpose. Don't forget that God gave favor to Esther before the eunuch so that she can be well dressed with costly ornaments to make her beautifully attractive to the king. Do you think God can give a man favor to break his rules for once? Have you seen or heard or read in the scripture that God gave favor to a man to go and fornicate or steal? Never! God did not ask the Hebrew to steal jewels of gold from the Egyptians. This was a true example of Him (God) blessing his people without causing them to sin in the process.

The Egyptians were in trouble that night because they lost their first born, even up to the animals, Moses could have asked the Hebrews to take whatever they see around but he said, ask your neighbor for gifts of gold and clothing because it is wrong to steal a thing that is not given to you. We teach against earrings but ask members to pay tithes of money they stole. Prostitutes pay tithes today in the church and we preach against earrings. Some remove their earrings when coming to the church and put it on at home; who then are you deceiving, God or yourself?

ESTHER PRAYED

David said, "if I regard iniquity in my heart thy Lord will not hear me, if gold rings were wrong and evil, then, why would Esther pray and God would hear her, Esther 4: 15–16.

Then Esther sent this answer to Mordecai go and get all the Jews in Susa together and fast for me three days and I will fast like you and my girl servants will fast too. Esther who put on gold rings and expensive ornaments fasted to God and God did answer her. Are you saying that Esther removed the ornaments before fasting? Let's even agree for a moment that she removed them, she must have had to wear it before appearing before the king. Does that then mean God can be mocked? No! God cannot be mocked. If something is wrong, then you must let it go and never return to it again. If Esther removed the jewels of gold then, she should not use it again and if removing it when praying and wearing it after is allowed, then, evil can be done before or after prayer but during prayer we shouldn't do it. God hates evil. You must not hold sins that provoke God in your heart and life. All your life and time must be used in holiness and not with impurity and hypocrisy.

Esther prayed and God answered because what she wore was not a problem. God said I judge by the intents of the heart. You may smile to deceive me but GOD will judge you by what goes on in your heart.

Job collected gold rings and God still said concerning him that he is a godly man, job 42: 7–10.

CHAPTER FIVE

DRESS MODESTY

I Timothy 2: 9

I also want women to wear clothes that are right for them. Women should dress with respect and right thinking. They should not use fancy braided hair or gold or pearls or expensive clothes to make themselves beautiful.

In Paul's letters to brother Timothy; he talked about women and their dressing. I am not going to talk about dresses now but if there is provision for the publishing then, I will. But Paul said "women should not use fancy braided hair or gold or pearls or expensive clothes. Could this perhaps be a source of the many misconceptions by

55

some preachers about gold and the use of it? Let us find out more on this statement.

WHY DID PAUL TALK ABOUT THIS?

The People of Ephesus were gentiles that believed in wrong doctrines and did not understand the ways of God. They saw the light through the message of the believers that went to them. They were into idolatry and prostitution before. They became believers in the TRUE LIGHT {JESUS}; but still need to be guided. Like Ezekiel 8: 17 talks about people wearing gold ring to honor the moons. These people worshipped strange things before but still dressed around to show their beauty just as before. They dressed to show people their beauty and also to seduce. Paul in his statement examined here need to show their beauty by the wearing of gold or pearls or costly array but make themselves beautiful by doing good things. In plain words, it's like saying you are a different person now; you do not belong to Ephesus where worshipping of Artemis is done but to a kingdom where worshipping of THE TRUE GOD IS ALLOWED AND good attitude is the garment.

Acts 19: 23–28

> (23)   But during that time, there was some bad trouble in Ephesus. This trouble was about the way of Jesus. This is how it all happened;

> (24)   There was a man named Demetrius. He worked with silver; he made little silver models that looked like the temple of the goddess Artemis (Diana).

> (26) But look at what this man Paul has influenced and changed many people. He has done this in Ephesus and all over the country of Asia.

Paul says the gods that men make are not real Artemis was a well-known Idol in the entire Asia and all the people traveled to worship it. They worship it by showing their body. Artemis was a goddess that was well designed and beautifully dressed hence the women dressed in like manner to show their beauty. Note that Paul did not send the letter to the people of Jerusalem but to the Ephesians because he knew their background and was asking the believing women not to daily look gorgeously dressed like they did to Artemis instead they should show their beauty by to wearing godliness which is showing the internal beauty with good attitude. Peter wrote letters to God's chosen people who are away from their homes, scattered all over the areas of Pontius, Galatia, Cappadocia, Asia and Bithynia. Peter also wrote on women respecting their husband and not let what they hold their husband with be that outward adorning of plaiting the hair and of wearing of gold or of putting on of apparel

WHY?

These women see only their beauty as the way to entice men and they so believed this, that, they do not like joke with looking good. They plait their hair as at when due and loved gold with all their heart because of the environmental religion and practices. The Apostles, however said, this is not what to show or preach to people. Let your husbands' see good attitude and respect such as you have not shown before and let people around see the new light you have seen that they may desire this and emulate your good and godly life.

DID PAUL CONDEMN GOLD RING?

I Timothy, 2: 9

They should not use fancy braided hair or gold or pearls or expensive clothes. He talks of three things here, braided hair, gold or expensive clothes. If gold here meant evil and that women should not use it then, braiding of hair [Irun didi] as we call it in Yoruba language is wrong. People that preach against gold from this chapter put on braids and also buy expensive clothes. They buy thousands of naira of clothes for burials and wedding ceremonies yet complain of gold. The verse also talks about expensive clothes. We use

Italian suits, we use expensive cars and live in big mansions; we should not let all these be our body or physical message to people around us.

The people Paul was sending the letter to used money to buy costly array to make them beautiful because it is what they do and believe in. It was a competition among them to wear what made them costly and appear valuable.

ARTEMIS LIKE METEORITE

Meteorite is a costly, very beautiful and very rare stone. They believed that Artemis looked like meteorite in appearance and shape. That is why they believed it is a

59

wealthy idol and the worshipers must be wealthily and beautifully dressed in such manner that they show their beauty by not putting on something that covers their body for seduction. Paul therefore said wear clothes that are right for you because you are a different person. How you have access to the LORD GOD and HE requires you to look good but not for immorality. Idols are nothing and those who worship it worship demons. 1 Cor. 10:19-20.

Satan rules and sends his fallen angels assignment to destroy Adam by making us GOD'S enemy. When you use your GOD given gift for evil then you are HIS enemy.

Adulterers can do and live any life, because Satan does not have a standard. Paul said you belong to GOD who has a standard.

WHAT CLOTHES ARE RIGHT FOR YOU?
Gen 3: 7

Then both the man and woman changed. It was like their eyes opened and they saw things differently. They saw that they had no clothes on them for they were naked. So they got some fig leaves and sewed them together and wore the fig leaves for clothes (verse21). The Lord God used animal skins and made some clothes for the man and his wife. Then he put the clothes or them.

God covered very well the nakedness of Adam and eve because they were not properly covered with fig leaves and God used animal skins that had no hole to view their nakedness to cover them.

But these people buy seductive clothes that made them look sexy, more beautiful for seduction and Paul said dress in a proper way, cover your nakedness and that is the mind of God and not stumbling men with your seductive dressing.

HOW DO YOU DRESS?

Do you wear gold ring because you want to look sexy, more beautiful? For God is not against you looking beautiful but not sexy.

Sexy means looking romantically attractive. When you dress mainly to attract men, you have wrong and evil motive for that and God will not be happy with that. A child of GOD should dress well and lets righteousness be what you gorgeously put on. Show it when you talk, walk and behave. Holiness is not rough dressing but keeping the commandments of God and living the will of GOD among the people.

CHAPTER SIX

YOUR ATTITUDE GLORIFIES GOD
1
Pet 3: 1–16

(1)   In the same way, you wives should be willing to serve your husband. Then if some of your husbands have not obeyed God's teaching. They will be persuaded to believe. You will not need to say anything. They will be persuaded by the way their wives live

(2)   Your husbands will see the pure lives that you live with your respect for God.

(3)   It is not fancy hair, gold jewelry, or expensive clothes that should make you beautiful. (4) Your beauty should come from inside you.

(5)   It was the same with the holy women who live long ago and follow God. They made themselves beautiful in that same way

(6)   I am talking about women like Sarah. She obeyed Abraham and called him master.

Peter wrote this letter to the brethren in Pontius, Galatia and Asia and he discussed in the letter about qualities of women that should be found in church. The letter corresponds to Paul's letter in 1Timothy 2 asking them to let godliness be their garment and not fancy hair, gold jewelry, or fine clothing. He says beauty should come from inside not outside. Peter used Sarah as an example that women should emulate. Let us briefly look at the life of Sarah

SARAH

Sarah, the wife of Abraham that called Abraham master and showed to the people around the right way for women to behave. Abraham's first gift to Rebecca;

Gen 24:1

(1)   Abraham lived to be a very old man, THE LORD blessed Abraham

(2)   Abraham's oldest servant was in charge of everything Abraham owned. Abraham called the servant to him and said, "Put your hand under my leg

(3)   Now I want you to make a promise to me before the Lord, the God of heaven and earth, that you will not allow my son to marry a girl from Canaan

(4)   Go back to my country to my own people. Find a wife for my son Isaac and bring her here to him.

Abraham wanted his son to marry a wife from his people. Abraham was careful of everything he does; he feared God so much and wouldn't want his son's wife to change him from following God. Abraham sent his chief servant and gave him gifts to give to whoever God sent to be his son's wife and gifts to the family.

Gen 24: 21-22

(21)   The servant quietly watched her. He wanted to be sure that the Lord had given him answer and had made his trip successful

(22)   After the camels finished drinking, he gave Rebecca a gold ring that weighed 1\4 ounce; he also gave her two gold arm bracelets that weigh 5 ounce each.

The gold ring and the bracelets were the first gifts given to Rebecca (Isaac's wife to be). Abraham made the chief servant to swear not to do anything contrary to his will. This implies that the chief servant's gift to Rebecca was part of Abraham decisions.

The chief servant now believed in the God of Abraham and does according to the practices he saw in Abraham. (Verse 12); the servant said, "LORD, you are the God of my master Abraham; allow me to find a wife for his son today. Please show this kindness to my master.

The man prayed to God not to idols. He did not need images of any form before he prayed. He said Lord, you are the God of my master and he placed down conditions to know the right person for Isaac. Verse 21 said he watched Rebecca to know if she was the answer to his prayer. This man believed in God that He answers prayers because he had seen him answering his master's prayers. The man believed in GOD and wouldn't rebel against his master's 'belief. Therefore, giving gold ring to Rebecca means that it was a message from Abraham.

REBECCA IN SARAH'S APARTMENT

Gen 24: 66–67

The servant told Isaac about all the things that had happened.

{6} then Isaac brought the girl into his mother's tent. Rebecca became Isaac wife that day. Isaac loved her very much, so Isaac was comforted after his mother death.

Rebecca lived in the tent of Sarah, her mother in-law. She did not go there herself but Isaac took her there. Abraham must know about this which means Abraham wanted to comfort Isaac for the death of his mother because he was lonely and he sent his chief servant to represent him because he is old. The gold ring and the arm bracelets show that the gold ring was not wrong. Abraham saw Rebecca and did not speak against the acts of his chief servant neither did he ask Rebecca to remove the bracelets.

Rebecca prayed Gen
25:22;

While Rebecca was pregnant, she had much trouble with the babies inside her. Rebecca prayed to the Lord and said why this happening to me?

GOD answered Rebecca's prayers without asking her to remove the gold ring and the bracelets she wore .If you are saying that Rebecca did not wear it when praying, then you are saying that GOD does not have problem with gold ring when used at home but must not be used in HIS presence. If gold ring is evil, it is wrong at home and in HIS presence {church} because GOD is everywhere.

SARAH'S GODLINESS

Since gold ring and bracelets were given to Rebecca, it is proved that Abraham did not use the bracelets but it must belong to Sarah. Yet Paul and peter wrote on how women should publicly behave not by showing fancy hair or gold ring and expensive clothes. Peter referring to Sarah does not mean that Sarah did not use gold ring but did not let that be the reason for living as a woman but to live a life pleasing to GOD and to be a good role model to women around and those coming behind.

Sarah was scripturally said to be a very beautiful woman. The king of Egypt noticed her at a very old age, also, the Amalekites' king also noticed her. Sarah was driven by her beauty yet she respected her husband and called him Lord. Christian women with beauty, influence and wealth fail to honor their husbands but Sarah did honor Abraham and called him master. She agreed that Abraham owns her and everything she had. Beloved, your attitude is what glorifies GOD.

Peter was saying, though Sarah had all it takes to be proud, being the first lady of Abraham. With 318 trained soldiers without counting the female and the children that lived with Sarah and Abraham, yet Sarah humbled herself and agrees with Abraham. She fulfilled the will of

GOD that says "wives honor your husbands."

CONCLUSION

Uses of ear ring is never the good news (Gospel) Christ asked us to preach. Satan in his evil way has taken away the Gospel from our lips and give us his own message.

Outer appearances deceived the ordinary eyes but not to a spirit man. During the ministry of Christ on earth, he never preached what we are preaching today on ear rings. Yet His three and half years of ministry were full of worthy teachings.

Brethren, we are not writing this to tell those who are not using ear ring to go to the market to buy neither do we tell those using ear ring that they won't make heaven but we are saying let there be moderation in everything we do.

Misconceptions on the usage of jewelries